wild voices

an anthology of short poetry & art by women

VOLUME 2

Copyright © 2018 Caroline Skanne

All rights revert to respective authors & artists upon publication. No work featured here may be used, copied, sold or distributed elsewhere without permission.

ISBN-13: 978-1985167353
ISBN-10: 1985167352

Published by
wildflower poetry press

www.wildflowerpoetrypress.wordpress.com

wildflowerpoetrypress@gmail.com

Front cover design: Caroline Skanne

Editor: Caroline Skanne

*Lock up your libraries if you like;
but there is no gate, no lock, no bolt that
you can set upon the freedom of my mind.*

—Virginia Woolf, *A Room of One's Own*

Editor's Note

The second volume of *wild voices* is a direct response to the success of the first volume published in 2017. In the vein of its predecessor, this year has collected over 70 contemporary voices in short poetry and art exploring aspects of women's experience. It is by no means a definite collection attempting to map out any leading names, but rather aims to provide a 'snapshot' of the short poem and closely related art, interpreted by women poets and artists around the world. The submissions received shaped this volume.

The call for submissions for this venture was prompted by the international women's day in 2016. With a background in anthropology and gender studies, my drive as an editor was to include work across the artistic community of the short poem, to provide a sample of expressions across the spectrum. The result is a celebration of not only the short poem and its many variations (ranging from haiku, senryu, tanka and closely related short form styles, to that of the micropoem and free verse poetry more broadly) but also, of the female voice in poetry and art, so often neglected or marginalised. the *wild voices* volumes attempt to somehow help readjust the imbalance, nothing more, nothing less.

I hope you will enjoy this year's helping of poetry and art, by some of the most exciting voices of the short poetry community, ranging from the experienced, to those new on the scene.

A warm thank you to the contributors in this book, as well as to the readers, you are all appreciated!

—Caroline Skanne, Editor

in the secret garden
where I left it,
my red cape

susan beth furst

a canyon wren sings
with a meandering stream
I sense hearts
of small hidden creatures
beating faster as I pass

weeding
around the ginkgo tree . . .
shadows of pterosaurs

sunlight sifts through summer maples a trail of emerald beetles

Mary Jo Balistreri

winter sky—
a juvenile buck
passes my window

scarecrow
dancing with sunflowers
the dorothy in me

Jill Lange

spring thaw
the heel of my boot
worn to the tack

Kelly Sauvage Angel

Penney Knightly

quietly joining
the conversation . . .
prairie stars

one of those days . . .
inviting a fly
in for tea

skipping my worry stone sinks

Julie Warther

fallen leaves . . .
the time I chose
another path

Eufemia Griffo

writing dark thoughts
in a colorful notebook

Olivia Dresher

Goodbye Maytree
After Annie Dillard

I summited the monument again today.
As I looked out over the ocean, over
the weary shacks and the dunes, I felt small.
This task of letting go,
of resisting bitterness and finding peace,
is something I can do.
It is not my failing when others find love.
It is not my flaws that cause others to leave.
I will climb this monument every day
until the work is done, until I am whole.
This is something I can do.
This is a task, a task of letting go.

Trish Hopkinson

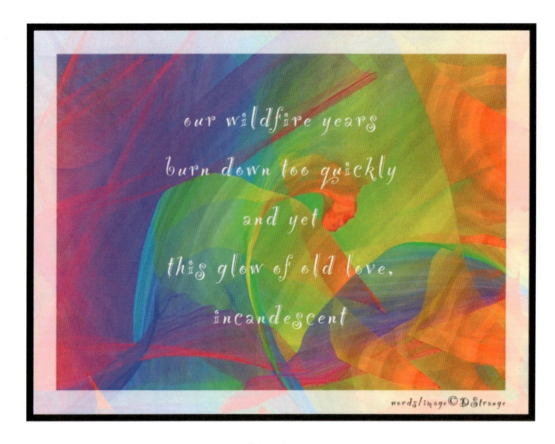

Debbie Strange

a twisted plum
scarred and knotted
blossoming
your imperfections
draw you to me

thunder snow
the cedars and i
kowtowing

he tells me
only part of the story—
sundog
a shard of glass
in the raven's beak

Marilyn Fleming

crossroads
we argue
about our direction

Louise Hopewell

grad school break . . .
yet another lover
in Kansas

old ducks out back
chase off the new ducks
I intrude
into a male profession
upsetting the pecking order

Pris Campbell

no room at the inn for a pregnant refugee

International Women's Day—
he rolls his eyes
like a rattled doll

they search for my cervix
  orchids on the ceiling

Helen Buckingham

Christine Stoddard

filling our silence
the heavy scent
of lilies

deep winter
knitting hours of darkness
in bright red yarn

lifelong illness
but still
these dreams

Rachel Sutcliffe

the zinnias
want to die
I keep watering

Erica Goss

lost in my darkness
tracing the edge
I crawl outward—
the slow navigation
to a swathe of stars

Joanna Ashwell

a solitary woman
knows a heartache
or two
tossing scarlet petals
into her evening bath

with blue irises
a woman in white
carries sorrow
down a path
nobody wants to go

Pamela A. Babusci

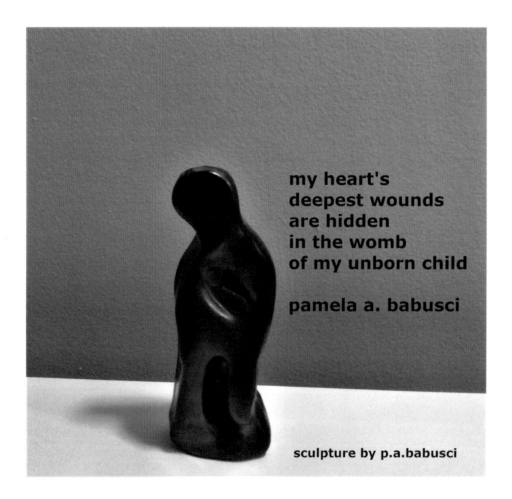

Pamela A. Babusci

the bird feeder
full of rain—
winter loneliness

pale blue sky deficient in my fifth chakra

Jessica Malone Latham

negative space
enough empty
for a flower

Caroline Skanne

Cellist in Winter

She wears ivory
to honor the snow

but not be a part of it.
Ivory, the color

of tusks and hairpins
that Heian poets used

to restrain a river
of black tresses—

for the cellist to counter
the melancholy chords

of the black keys while
playing Boccherini.

She holds her bow
like a calligrapher

brushing wisps of sound,
pulses from the heart

of a solitary gull
released into sky.

Margaret Chula

by the river
twilight envelops
a white stork

Nina Kovačić
transl. *Đurđa Vukelić Rožić*

night bus
her tattoo flies away
with each street light

cloudless sunset
across the horizon
a necklace of birds

Iliyana Stoyanova

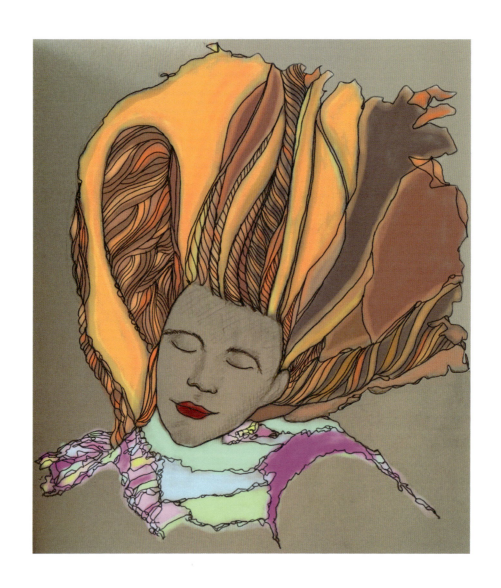

Penney Knightly

talking with mom
about my first period
white pleated skirt

crêpes suzette
he rarely gives
flowers

Claire Vogel Camargo

on the summer solstice
skinny dipping
in the Gihon River
   jingle of bracelets
   my quickening heart

Margaret Chula

flow—
my father always said
what's the hurry

birthplace
beside the playground
an adult pine

Kerstin Park

medicinal plant walk—
the dog fetches the stick
then eats it

sparrows compete
with church bells
Sunday in Tuscany

kjmunro

her bony back
against my palm—
Mother's Day

this corn cooking
in the time it takes
to sing a song

fifty-something:
the birthday book of my youth
used for deaths now too

Maeve O'Sullivan

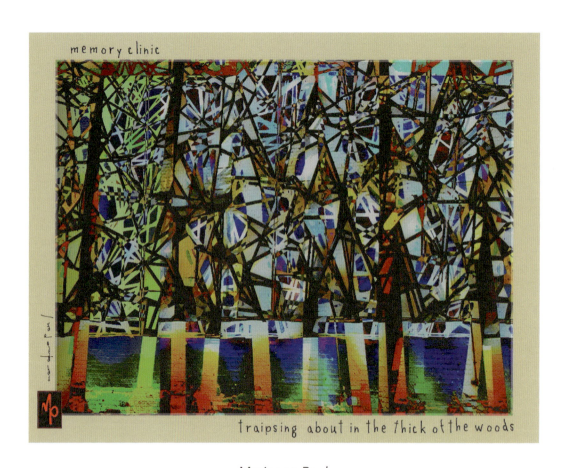

Marianne Paul

left on the fridge
at the bottom of the
to-do-list
bury me
next to the baby

yesterday
my son mowed the grass
for the first time
our yard
has crop circles

watching him
fall out of love with me
over the years
the missing sock bin fills
then overflows

Susan Burch

a red dawn blazes
from charcoal banked at twilight
embers of my dreams
waver in the morning chill
between sunlight and shadow

pine shadows lengthen
as a blue heron hunches
over gray waters
distorted by thunder clouds
I stand without reflection

Elizabeth Spencer Spragins

her palms
bruising cardamom seeds
the subtleties of chai

mom's hair
tied in a chignon . . .
candles lit
for refugees

no play-dates
or scheduled layovers
@humantrafficking

Jan Benson

Moss in the Grass

The dark moss seeps like floodwater through our ragged lawn, swallowing the last clumps of neglected grass, and still hungry. Always hungry. We're told moss signals disease, but moss poison is expensive and we don't believe in it. Anyway we are tired. The spreading moss becomes a thick carpet that sinks sympathetically under our feet. In early spring, tiny yellow flowers bloom like match flames. Spindly dandelions and purple clover come next. By fall, a wild forest floor surrounds the house, and the neighbors start to look away. Young rabbits come at dusk and grackles gather in the morning. A branch falls from the old oak tree, almost killing one of us, and the retaining wall crumbles in the rain. If the hunt isn't allowed, the newspaper says, black bears will be coming soon from the mountains. We say, let them come.

Ann Malaspina

mazed as a stoat

she is
mazed as a stoat
hissing, spitting,
fast and furious
across the dark moor

she fears
nothing, no predator,
no man
gold and silver
will not tempt her

she is wild
and cannot be tamed
by any love
she has no time
for romance

she races
with the south wind
alone
in bleak places
where the thorn trees grow

she tosses
her red hair back
and runs away
into the night and sits
snarling, by the fire

Joy McCall

Marianne Paul

deep sea emotions we sight a blue whale

a way of swans we drift

pink strewn seaweed no apologies for passion

Robyn Cairns

whiskey flavour . . .
the seductive taste
of my remorse

moonless night—
a lullaby
of lies

Maria Laura Valente

coming out
I tell my grandchildren
I'm a poet

mammogram
dropping my shirt
for a stranger

Marianne Paul

long weekend . . .
the cat and I
both sleep late

Mary Gunn

Gaia Woolf-Nightingall

warm brandy
her shadow removes
another garment

Margaret Rutley

moonlit hair . . .
un-braiding
our legs

Sidney Bending

in the limo
the bride reties
a tennis shoe

chemo
the passport photo
no longer me

Barbara Tate

tossing turning
waking up
to nightmares

peeling tree bark
she hides her spotted hands
in the interview

Amy Losak

scrape of steel wool
against the casserole pan . . .
I break a promise

pick-your-own—
my daughter chases a boy
through the strawberry fields

cumulocirrus—
the best part of my day
cloud gazing with you
in the preschool
parking lot

calling home
such unexpected frailty
in my mother's voice
I begin to wear
her perfume

Julie Bloss Kelsey

Pat Davis

let me live
in a moss green cottage
stained by
lichen and raindrops where
my heart beats with birdsong

wearing
her neon blue boots
she soars
into 70
a wrecked tornado

spinning
always toward
the light

Carole Johnston

tell me something good.

before bed, mother traced words into my back.
she wrote *beautiful. brave. baby. love.*
i tried to guess them & was usually wrong,
so she voiced them to me, low & resonant—
lullabies sung to me before i existed outside of her.

Leigh Cheak

slow falling snow
all the lessons
I wish to unlearn

desktop
my messy life
in neat folders

dappled light
between faith and doubt
I rest my feet

Debbi Antebi

Gaia Woolf-Nightingall

Jörmungandr

Down there, ocean-circling,
rolling over your own head
the way a ring slips off the table,
spins between two people – you
are how we know we've already
bitten ourselves in the ass.

We are careful not to argue, not
to glimpse your roiling; you
surface, sink, worry episodic
memory from our sleep, gleaming
through the thrust-moraines
and fjords of our gyri,

the doom in our limbic system,
Sigurd-snake-in-the-eye hidden
between the chromosomes,
you dream your end-time dreams.
Stay down. We don't want
to hear it's already over.

Sonja Johanson

watching the cormorant dive . . .
how long can I hold my breath?

unpicking
the family story
one lie at a time

staring
into the mirror
wondering
which one of us
will look away first

Karen Harvey

cracked asphalt
the wildflower and i
both hopeful

replacing the idea of you with anything else

among the what-ifs a voice i can't place

Shloka Shankar

Barbara Kaufmann

stepping off a boat
and onto Ellis Island,
you changed your name—
writing the first page
of your new life

wisteria finds
a new path no matter
what is cut away—
if only you realized
there was a choice

a single blossom
on the old gardenia . . .
looking in the mirror
and seeing
only myself

Mary Kendall

after the fall
healing by
juniper berry

ancient cedars on the
Niagara Escarpment
I listen for stories

Leslie Bamford

when I'm not looking
green bud
red bud

*when the bow breaks
refugees drift
on the tide*

Gail Oare

five of us
under the large umbrella
her grave

dawn echoes
the earth's silence
High Sierra

her forgetfulness
blueberries roll under
the refrigerator

Deborah P Kolodji

a fledgling
on my balcony
oh, mother
i need you today
more than yesterday

Debbie Strange

hospice sunrise
a smile of recognition
through the mist

four-handed clock . . .
we wind
grandma's wool
stretching the night
towards solstice

Martha Magenta

morning sun
on my wrinkles
and your scars -
our bodies
telling stories

Leslie Bamford

between lovers
searching for mushrooms
in the woods

Lee Nash

stargazing
a moment alone
with my ancestors

the anniversary
of mother's passing
heavy rain

Tiffany Shaw-Diaz

booze run

and the octogenarian aunties arrive and one settles into a pink flowered nightie and hair curlers and the other's in a grey sweatsuit and they send me to the liquor store—vodka and tomato juice for the one with hair curlers *and cheap hooch whiskey* croaks the sweatsuit auntie and mom says *get bourbon for mint juleps—we're from kentucky, remember?* and the air is cracker crisp and tall paper bags crunch and the aunties curl up and swill their drinks and the sweatsuit auntie swigs down her vitamin pills

sisters together
for the last time
laughter of autumn leaves

Jennifer Hambrick

cumulus clouds
she puffs a cigarette
at the graveyard gate

browning tulips
pink lace panties
at the side of the road

her paycheck
next to his
three-quarter moon

Jennifer Hambrick

Christine Stoddard

i travel
by helicopter
in the canyon
a shaman's song
as the eagle soars

the wolves you hear
the wolves i hear
this night
of love
dying

river moon
a song for the dead
on the other side

ai li

five languages
at 95 she talks in her sleep
to each child

winter chill
why must I walk so far
to meet the moon

midnight blue
the last flower I put
in her white hair

for my mother (1920 - 2015)

Kath Abela Wilson

a child
gazes across the river
to distant hills
blushing with springtime
an old woman gazes back

a swirl
of alabaster silk
among the pines . . .
a wraith of music rises,
smoke from an empty hearth

moss grows green
where the stream cuts deep
I seek
a blessing from the roots
that bind it all together

Jenny Ward Angyal

Publication Credits

Mary Jo Balistreri, 'sunlight sifts . . .', *hedgerow #80*

Jill Lange, 'scarecrow', *Failed Haiku, November, 2016*

Jill Lange, 'winter sky', *Modern Haiku, 47:3*

Julie Warther, ' quietly joining', *2016 Betty Drevniok Award, Honorable Mention*

Julie Warther, 'one of those days . . .', *Art of Haiku, May 2016 semi-finalist*

Julie Warther, 'skipping my worry stone sinks', *hedgerow #91*

Eufemia Griffo, ' fallen leaves', *Failed Haiku, Vol. 2, Issue 22, 2017*

Trish Hopkinson, 'Goodbye Maytree', *#thesideshow*

Marilyn Fleming, 'a twisted plum', *Blithe Spirit, Autumn, 2016*

Marilyn Fleming, 'thunder snow', *Akitsu Quarterly, December, 2016*

Marilyn Fleming, 'he tells me', *Tanka Society of America 2016 Anthology*

Helen Buckingham, 'no rom . . .', *Brass Bell, March, 2017*

Helen Buckingham, 'International Women's Day', *Presence 49*

Helen Buckingham, 'they search for my cervix', *Modern Haiku 43, 2, 2012*

Pamela A. Babusci, 'a solitary woman', *A Solitary Woman, 2013*

Pamela A. Babusci, 'with blue irises', *A Solitary Woman, 2013*

Nina Kovačić, transl. Đurđa Vukelić Rožić, 'by the river', *Iris Magazine*

Iliyana Stoyanova, 'night bus', *Second Place in the 16th edition of the European Quarterly Kukai, December, 2016*

Iliyana Stoyanova, 'cloudless sunset', *Third Prize in the 22nd "Kusamakura" International Haiku Competition, 18 November 2017*

Claire Vogel Camargo, 'talking with mom', *Brass Bell, March, 2017*

Claire Vogel Camargo, 'crêpes suzette', *Brass Bell, April, 2017*

Margaret Chula, 'on the summer solstice', *Just This, Mountains & Rivers Press, 2013*

Kerstin Park, 'flow', *Failed Haiku, March, 2017*

Kerstin Park, 'birthplace', *Failed Haiku, January, 2017*

Maeve O'Sullivan, 'her bony back', Winner of Haiku Ireland Kukai #20, 2010; anthologised in "evolution", Red Moon anthology of English-language haiku in 2010, published in 2011; Initial Response, 2011, Alba Publishing

Maeve O'Sullivan, 'this corn cooking', *Blithe Spirit*, Issue 23/3; selected to be anthologised in *Frogpond*, Issue 37:1, March, 2014; *A Train Hurtles West*, Alba Publishing, 2015

Maeve O'Sullivan, 'fifty-something', *Abridged*, April 2016; *Elsewhere*, Alba Publishing, 2017

Susan Burch, 'left on the fridge', *Frameless Sky*, November, 2015

Susan Burch, 'yesterday', *Bamboo Hut*, December, 2013

Susan Burch, 'watching him', *A Hundred Gourds*, 2014

Jan Benson, 'her palms', *Blithe Spirit*, 26.4

Jan Benson, 'mom's hair', *Path to Peace Anthology*, September, 2016

Jan Benson, 'her palms', *Blithe Spirit*, 26.4

Jan Benson, 'no play-dates', *hedgerow #99*

Joy McCall, 'mazed as a stoat', *Atlas Poetica*, issue 21

Margaret Rutley, 'warm brandy', *Erotic Haiku of skin on skin*, 2017

Sidney Bending, 'moonlit hair', *Erotic Haiku of skin on skin*, 2017

Amy Losak, 'peeling tree bark', *the International Women's Haiku Festival*, 2016

Julie Bloss Kelsey, 'scrape of steel wool', *Modern Haiku 43:3*

Julie Bloss Kelsey, ' pick-your-own', *Gnarled Oak*, Issue 3

Julie Bloss Kelsey, 'cumulocirrus', *Bright Stars, An Organic Tanka Anthology*, Vol. 5

Julie Bloss Kelsey, 'calling home', *Moonbathing 14*

Sonja Johanson, 'Jörmungandr', *Redheaded Stepchild*

Jennifer Hambrick, 'booze run', *Haibun Today*, Vol. 10, No. 4

Jennifer Hambrick, 'her paycheck', *Modern Haiku*, 48.2

ai li, 'i travel', *Raw NerVZ Haiku Vol. VII, No.1 Summer*

ai li, 'the wolves you hear', *Raw NerVZ Haiku Vol. VI, No.3, Fall*

ai li, 'river moon', *Modern Haiku Vol. XXX, No 3*

Made in the USA
Columbia, SC
13 March 2018